Original title:
The Bramble Diaries

Copyright © 2025 Creative Arts Management OÜ
All rights reserved.

Author: Giselle Montgomery
ISBN HARDBACK: 978-1-80567-200-5
ISBN PAPERBACK: 978-1-80567-499-3

Portrait of Resilience in the Thorns

In a garden full of prickly jokes,
Laughter dances where no one pokes.
Each thorn a tale, each leaf a grin,
Resilient blooms beneath the din.

With tangled roots that twist and twine,
Whispering secrets over the vine.
A comedy of errors and light,
In this happy mess, we take flight.

Lament of the Wayward Stem

Oh, the stem that couldn't choose,
A path of daisies or vibrant blues.
It zigged and zagged, lost its way,
In pursuit of sunshine, come what may.

With each direction, a chance to flail,
Bumping into weeds with a comical wail.
A fragile giggle in the wind's embrace,
Even lost, it finds a joyful space.

A Pathway Clothed in Shadows

Underneath the leafy shroud,
Whispers chuckle, laughter loud.
Shadows stretch with playful grace,
While flowers giggle in this place.

Twisting roots in a game of peek,
Silly secrets, shy and sleek.
They weave through darkness, a cheeky dance,
In this hidden nook, they take a chance.

The Language of Intertwined Stems

In a tangle of words, they entwine,
Sassy banter that's simply divine.
Each stem a story, bold and spry,
With punchlines poking the passersby.

Their leafy tongues in a playful duel,
A comedy act on nature's stool.
Together they flourish, a riotous crew,
In the whispers of green, laughter ensues.

Ascent Through the Twisted Garden

In a garden tangled tight,
Bumblebees hold their flight.
Caterpillars wear tiny crowns,
While the daisies giggle, bouncing down.

I climbed a vine, oh what a feat!
Tripped on roots beneath my feet.
Thorns poked fun, I stomped and slipped,
In this leafy world, I fumbled and flipped.

Rabbits watch with sly old grins,
While I tumble, do my spins.
A snail raced by, I cheered it on,
In this wild maze, I felt like a fawn.

With every turn, I spot a friend,
Nature's jest seems without end.
Laughter echoes through the green,
In this quirky place, I'm a silly queen.

Songs of the Resilient Vine

In the shade where the wild things grow,
Sings a vine, all tangled and slow.
With leaves that whisper jokes and pranks,
It tickles the air, while nature wanks.

Bugs hold a concert, cacophonous cheer,
They boogie and spin, causing a stir.
A ladybug hops, calling a tune,
While shadows dance beneath the moon.

I caught a breeze that laughed as it blew,
Wrapped in the vines, like nature's goo.
Frogs croaked verses, off-key and loud,
Yet celebrated, we formed a crowd.

Together they sang, a symphony bright,
In the vibrant mess, all felt right.
With every chuckle, I felt so free,
In this wild garden, come sing with me!

Captured in the Grip of Nature

Trapped in roots, a tangled plight,
Where sunlight giggles, soft and bright.
Dandelions poke out their heads,
While ants march by in their stylish threads.

Caught in a grip, I start to sway,
The breeze plays games, leads me astray.
Thorns quipped at my flowery crown,
While grasshoppers chuckled, never a frown.

In bushes thick, shy critters peek,
While I chatter, they quietly sneak.
A squirrel nods, with peanuts to share,
In this thicket, we laugh without care.

Snapdragons snicker with colorful flair,
Wrapped in nature, beyond all compare.
The wildness enchants, I can't help but grin,
In the grip of this fun, I feel I must win!

The Unfolding of Green Shadows

Shadows stretch, leafy arms sway,
In tangled thickets, we laugh and play.
Beneath the boughs that twist and curl,
Nature's mischief makes my heart whirl.

A raccoon stumbles, wearing a hat,
Losing a game of catch with a cat.
The ferns are dancing, how they tease,
Swaying softly in the teasing breeze.

Roots weave laughter through chatter and cheer,
Each branch a friend, bringing good cheer.
A butterfly winks, fluttering sly,
As I trip and tumble, oh me, oh my!

With every step, wonder grows wide,
In this garden where secrets reside.
Through whispers of green, escapades unfold,
In nature's embrace, we dance bold and gold.

Symphony of the Twisted Woods

In tangled paths, we dance and sway,
A waltz of thorns that leads astray.
The trees hum tunes, both crisp and clear,
While squirrels plot mischief, oh dear!

With every dip, a giggle bursts,
A rustling sound, the laughter first.
Mice play drums on hollow logs,
Our concert disrupted by rambunctious frogs!

Leaves confetti in breezy glee,
As woodland creatures join the spree.
With each wrong turn, a new delight,
Who knew the woods could be so bright?

So grab your friends, let's make some noise,
In nature's realm, we're all just boys.
Bramble paths and silly tricks,
A symphony of laughter, let's fix!

Resonance of the Wild

Where shadows creep and giggles fly,
A parrot learns to mimic a sigh.
The hedgehogs roll, a clumsy dance,
While rabbits hop in a wild prance.

Nature's echo, a warm embrace,
In every corner, a funny face.
The owls whoop, "It's all a joke!"
As branches tickle, they softly choke.

Adventures bloom in tangled vines,
With maze-like paths, where mischief twines.
"Did you trip?!" a mischievous crow,
While flowers giggle in the afterglow.

So rush along, the wild awaits,
With wacky signs of nature's fates.
In this resonance, we find our tune,
With raucous laughter from sun to moon.

The Lattice of Untamed Wishes

In wild designs, our dreams unwind,
A lattice weaving fun combined.
The beetles march in silly rows,
While grasshoppers boast about their shows.

The foxes boast of clever tricks,
Their laughter ringing like music picks.
With every twist, a prank unfolds,
A nutty tale that never scolds.

Caterpillars dream of heights to reach,
While butterflies teach them what they breach.
In this chaotic, vibrant play,
We craft our wishes in a funny way.

So come and join the laughter loud,
In this lattice, we stand proud.
With every wish, a kooky dance,
Embracing wildness in our chance.

Epistles of the Unruly Wilderness

In letters sent by silly breeze,
A misfit tale of nature's tease.
The crickets chirp a comical tune,
While wildflowers argue 'neath the moon.

Each gust of wind, a playful jest,
From squirrel scholars at their best.
With scrolls of grass and ink of dew,
Nature writes secrets just for you.

The awkward dance of clumsy deer,
Makes every stroll feel full of cheer.
In this wild space, we pen our song,
With every laugh, we can't go wrong.

So read the notes from trees so tall,
In unruly love, we stand enthralled.
For in these epistles, pure delight,
We weave our magic through the night.

An Odyssey Through Twisted Paths

In a thicket where giggles sway,
Branches tickle in a playful way.
Bumbles and stumbles, oh what a sight,
Lost in this maze, oh what a delight!

Squirrels chatter, a comical crew,
Gathering nuts while making a stew.
Roots twist and turn, like an old dance,
Every wrong step feels like a chance!

The hedgehogs gossip, with snickers and grins,
Whispering secrets about their thick skins.
One twirls away, a show-off for sure,
Flipping and flopping, like he's on tour!

And as sunlight dips, shadows grow long,
We stumble and giggle, setting the tone.
Twisted and tangled, this journey seems bright,
An odyssey wrapped in laughter and light!

Voices Among the Tangle

In the bushes where voices collide,
A frog croaks a tune, starts the wild ride.
Whispers and chuckles, a creature parade,
A cacophony blooming, all unafraid.

The sly little fox, with a wink and a jest,
Tells tales of grand quests that never did rest.
Each phrase a riddle, each laugh a delight,
As we tumble together, what a funny sight!

Rabbits hop by with a bounce and a flair,
Sharing their romps, without any care.
Underneath brambles, there's mischief afoot,
The laughter grows louder, roots tangled in loot!

When dusk settles softly, the giggles remain,
Voices among the tangle, never in vain.
With a wink to the stars, another day's quest,
In this joyful chaos, we're truly blessed!

Chronicles of Nature's Embrace

In the heart of green, where mayhem does bloom,
A butterfly flutters, spelling out doom.
A caterpillar shouts, 'I'm ready to fly!'
But under the brambles, it's all just a lie.

A worm wiggles past, with stories to tell,
Of misadventures under the soil's shell.
He chuckles and chirps, 'Take care where you crawl!'
In this nature's embrace, there's laughter for all!

The loopy old trees share tales, quite absurd,
Of squirrels who dance and forget every word.
Each leaf carries whispers of fun and delight,
In this tangled-up playground, everything's bright!

Under the chaos, friendships unfold,
Every twist in the path adds warmth to the cold.
These chronicles written in giggles and grins,
In nature's embrace, every misstep wins!

Serenade of Lost Footsteps

In a world of thorns, where shadows do creep,
Lost footsteps linger, but giggles still leap.
The hedges hide tales of mishaps and fun,
As we weave through the maze, joy has begun!

A wobbly snail leaves a shiny, sly trail,
While ants march in line, wearing tiny mail.
With every misstep and tumble we share,
The serenade plays on, beyond any care!

The sky's painted gold, with clouds made of fluff,
We dance as we dodge all the prickles and stuff.
Every twist in our path sings out loud, there's cheer,
In the serenade of lost steps, we have no fear!

As twilight approaches, we count our mistakes,
Each wrong turn we take adds to our shakes.
With laughter we echo through the night's gentle glow,
In this funny adventure, let's just go with the flow!

Constellations of Leaf and Thorn

In a garden of chaos, I roam with glee,
Bramble sticks poke like they're trying to flee.
Where thorns laugh loud, and leaves dance on air,
Hey, watch your step! It's a prickly affair.

Sunshine sizzles with the odd buzzing bee,
Buzzing past flowers, they're all wild and free.
Underbrush giggles as I stumble and slide,
Through nature's riddle, it's a fun little ride.

I tiptoe through brambles like a circus act,
A pair of old boots, they have a pact.
Cherishing mischief that lives in each vine,
Wrestle the bushes—it's a joy divine!

With a wink from the daisies, I dance on my way,
Each thorn whispers secrets that make me want to stay.
In this granular jungle where chaos reigns,
Adventure and laughter are what remains.

Threads of Life in the Briar Patch

Within thorny chambers, I weave my new tale,
Sliding through green threads like a clumsy snail.
Spiderwebs shimmer, a glint in the sun,
Calling the laughter 'Hey, look, I've won!'

Looping and tangling, I laugh at my plight,
'Look at me, folks!' as I dance with delight.
Each misstep a giggle, each scratch a good cheer,
In this raucous adventure, I've nothing to fear.

The bumblebee chorus hums tunes of my fate,
Where thorns make a curtain—oh, isn't that great?
A pirouette here, and a twirl just for fun,
Who knew such chaos could be so well spun?

In the heart of the briars, life's tangled and sweet,
A mishap in stitches makes for a grand feat.
We're all just a thread in nature's wild patch,
Sewing up laughter as we dance in the scratch.

Nectar of the Wistful Bramble

Oh, taste the delight of a berry so bright,
Nestled in brambles, what a curious sight!
With each little nibble, my worries take flight,
A burst of sweet laughter in the soft twilight.

The thicket's a treasure, a puzzling fate,
Finding snack-sized gems that make all the late.
Fingers all sticky, I wave at a friend,
'Join in the fun until daylight does end!'

Bushes tell stories—each leaf has a grin,
Whispers of mischief that tease from within.
With nectar on lips, I dance with the breeze,
And summon the joy that flows through the trees.

Stumbling through brambles, embracing my plight,
Each pod filled with magic shines out like a light.
In a patch of wild wonders, laughter takes flight,
Sipping the nectar, everything feels right.

Carved by Nature's Hands

Amidst the wild thorns where adventure takes hold,
I'm a jester of nature, a tale to be told.
Each twig's a comedian, each root puns along,
Join me in laughter where we all belong.

The breeze has a giggle as it tickles my ear,
Quirky little creatures are drawing me near.
I trip on my laces; the trees shake their leaves,
'You're managing chaos, just see what it achieves!'

We're sculpted by whimsy, chaos, and fun,
With nature as artist, we all sing as one.
In brambles of mischief, life's a rollicking show,
Every twist of the vine adds a new little glow.

So here in the wild, where the laughter is grand,
We dance with delight, being sculpted by hand.
In this patchwork of joy, all worries dissolve,
With vibes of hilarity, our spirits involve!

Tangled Tales of Nature's Heart

In a tangle of leaves, I found a shoe,
A squirrel proudly hoarded it, who knew?
With acorns and twigs as precious loot,
It danced on branches, looking so cute.

The berries were ripe, but oh so sly,
Each bite brought a squawk, oh my, oh my!
The bees were buzzing a tune so sweet,
While ants had a parade, rhythmic and neat.

Thorned Memories and Summer Blooms

Thorns and blooms in a curious race,
A rose with attitude, a sassy face!
It called upon daisies, all in a fuss,
'Why do you all look so plain and fussed?'

The flowers would giggle, rolling in glee,
Making fun of the plants, as bold as can be.
Until the thorns whispered, 'Oh, my dear,
Without my sharp style, you'd disappear!'

The Dance of Twisting Roots

Roots wiggled and jiggled beneath the earth,
Competing for space, their own little turf.
'Can you believe what that tree just said?'
'It's all bark and no bite,' one root jokingly spread.

They whispered of dreams of rising so high,
While dodging the gnomes that passed them by.
A twig turned to a fern with a fabulous flair,
Twisting in rhythm, a forest affair!

A Gaze Through the Green

In the shade of a bush, a critter did peek,
With a mischievous grin, it started to squeak.
'Why do daisies always look so surprised?
They bloom in the sun, yet seem so disguised!'

With the wind giggling softly through the leaves,
A chorus of laughter that never deceives.
The mushrooms all chuckled, their caps in a row,
Whispering secrets of grass down below.

Reflections from the Untamed Verge

In the garden where weeds conspire,
A dandelion wears a furry attire.
The rabbits dance with wild delight,
As squirrels practice for the next night.

There's mischief brewed in the brush,
With ladybugs making quite the fuss.
They roll like balls, with shells so round,
In the wild chaos, joy is found.

A snail speeds by, a sight to see,
Wearing shades and sipping sweet tea.
The blooms gossip, their petals flail,
While worms write letters, long and frail.

The hedgehogs hold a game of tag,
Running laps where no one can brag.
Beneath the thorns, laughter takes flight,
In this overgrown, silly delight.

Fables from the Overgrown Realm

Once upon a time in a bramble patch,
A crow had dreams of being a match.
With feathers frayed and beak held high,
He practiced tricks, oh my, oh my!

A tortoise named Bert wore a tiny crown,
Hoping to win a slowpoke showdown.
But he tripped over grass, never was quick,
The sprightly hare laughed, oh what a trick!

A grasshopper played tunes on a leaf,
His band of crickets brought comic relief.
In this meadow of merriment and cheer,
Even the bushes joined in with a jeer.

When the sun bowed low in an orange blaze,
The critters danced in a wild craze.
Bramble tales that tickle the ear,
In this overgrown realm, there's nothing to fear!

Unraveled Tales of the Green Abyss

In the green abyss, where secrets are spun,
A cat's out of luck when he tries to run.
He chased a butterfly, oh what a chase,
But fell in a bush, it's a wild place!

The mushrooms held a midnight ball,
Toadstools dancing, oh how they did sprawl!
A frog in a tux, he croaked with glee,
"Who needs a prince? Just waltz with me!"

Beneath the brambles, a gossiping bee,
Whispering tales: "Did you see? Did you see?"
The ivy giggled, the vines intertwined,
In this tangled fun, mischief aligned.

As the moon peeked down, casting its light,
The thicket chuckled deep into the night.
Tales unraveled with each little twirl,
In this green abyss, life's quite a whirl!

Threads of Life in the Thicket

In the thicket where life's tangled threads,
   A hedgehog dreams in his cozy beds.
He knits tiny scarves from leaves of green,
   Fashionably late for the next unseen.

A rabbit had plans for a sorcerer's show,
With carrot wands that would dazzle and glow.
He pulled off tricks that left others gaped,
   Turning his friends into vegetables draped!

The wildflowers giggled, each bloom a delight,
   As bees buzzed around in their dizzy flight.
They painted the air with colors so bright,
   In this thicket of laughter, all felt just right.

As dusk draped the land in a silken thread,
The creatures whispered soft things before bed.
Life's woven closely, yet loose, like a game,
In this fun-filled thicket, we're all just the same!

Thorned Tales of the Forest

In the woods where prickles grow,
A rabbit tripped and stole the show,
He danced and hopped right on a vine,
The thorns just laughed, said, "We're fine!"

A squirrel tried to play it cool,
But got his tail stuck in a pool,
He splashed around like a crazy fish,
And made a frog go, "What a wish!"

A hedgehog wearing a tiny hat,
Knew all the secrets—imagine that!
He'd roll on by with quite the flair,
While brushing off the leaves and hair.

So if you wander near those trees,
Expect surprises with every breeze,
For in this forest, fun unfolds,
With prickly friends and tales retold.

In the Shadow of Gnarled Roots

Beneath the roots, where shadows creep,
A crafty fox made sure to leap,
He played hide and seek with a crow,
But lost the game—oh, what a show!

The owl hooted, "What a sight!",
As critters danced with sheer delight,
A band of bees with tiny hats,
Wove music through the giggling brats.

A tortoise claimed he knew the way,
While turtles laughed and joined the fray,
But went so slow, they missed the fun,
While fireflies blinked, "We're faster, run!"

So in the shadows, laughter thrives,
Where every twist is filled with jives,
These roots hold tales of joy and cheer,
In a forest where fun's always near.

Memoirs of the Enchanted Thicket

In thickets dense with leaves so thick,
A clumsy bear got stuck, oh what a trick!
He tried to find his way back home,
But ended up in a ladybug dome.

A wise old toad told jokes all night,
While dancing mushrooms donned their light,
They twirled and spun in sheer delight,
A ball of fun under the moonlight.

A family of raccoons stole a pie,
And tried to run, oh my, oh my!
But fumbled and spilled it with a thump,
While singing tunes, they made a jump.

These memoirs told of silly scenes,
Where forest friends were kings and queens,
So if you hear the laughter flow,
Join in the fun—they'll steal the show!

The Tangle of Forgotten Dreams

Among the brambles, dreams run wild,
A dreamy cat acted like a child,
He chased the shadows, jumped with glee,
While bumping into a busy bee.

A chatty parrot raved about a trip,
Yet tangled up on a viney grip,
He squawked, "Help! I'm stuck like glue!"
The other birds just laughed and flew.

A sleepy sloth thought it was a race,
He dawdled along, in his own slow pace,
The crowd cheered, but he didn't care,
He stretched, yawned, and took a chair.

In this tangle of dreams so bold,
Where life is funny and never old,
The whispers of the woods hold schemes,
Of laughter, fun, and silly dreams.

Thorns and Encounters

In a patch where the thistles grow,
I stumbled on a singing crow.
He laughed at my tangled hair,
I wondered if he'd ever care.

A hedgehog danced with nary a clue,
Wearing spikes like a fancy shoe.
He waved his paws, a spiky delight,
And rolled away, out of my sight.

A rabbit laughed, chewing on grass,
Said, "This thicket's a wild, funny class!"
I joined in the feast; it was a sight,
To share bites with battles of might.

Sunset painted the leaves in hues,
We twirled and stumbled with silly views.
In this bristly land of joy and cheer,
Friendship blooms where hearts don't fear.

The Heartbeat of Overgrown Dreams

In tangled vines, dreams sneak and play,
A squirrel's acrobat, what a display!
He crashed through branches, a wild ballet,
And winked at me as he made his way.

Among the blooms, a bee declared,
"Take care, my friend, I'm unprepared!"
He buzzed about like a winding kite,
While I clutched my snacks, ready for flight.

The flowers giggled, with petals aglow,
As I tripped on roots, a clumsy show.
A charming mess, this leafy dream,
In laughter, we floated, a silly team.

Beneath the canopy, we shared our plight,
A misfit gathering, a joyful sight.
With whispers of dreams and silly schemes,
We planted our hearts in overgrown beams.

Whispers of the Unruly Thicket

In the depths of the thicket's snare,
A fox held court with debonair flair.
With a twirl and a leap, he chose his tale,
Of sneaky snacks and a shiny trail.

A badger, with swagger, joined the fray,
"I found a dessert on my detour today!"
He licked his chops, a mischievous grin,
As crumbs of adventure danced in the din.

A pair of owls hooted with glee,
"Nothing beats this raucous spree!"
They perched above, sipping moonlight brew,
Giving wise advice without a clue.

In this unruly realm we found,
Laughter echoed, a joyful sound.
We celebrated our wild ballet,
In whispers that made the thicket sway.

Echoes of the Earthbound

In a forest deep, where shadows blend,
I met a turtle with time to spend.
He told me tales in a drawling tone,
Of adventures long and the seeds he'd sown.

The earthworms giggled beneath the ground,
Plotting mischief without a sound.
With wiggly dances, they declared their rules,
Teaching the trees a thing or two of jewels.

A snail brushed by, all shiny and slow,
"Life's not a race, just take it slow!"
With a giggle and a wink, he slipped away,
While I burst into giggles, brightening the gray.

Caught in this mischievous, earthy affair,
We spun wild tales with laughter to share.
Echoes of joy, through the roots they wound,
In this clay-slicked home where warm hearts abound.

Bramble Dreams and Sunlit Paths

In a garden where brambles grow,
The hedgehogs dance, all in a row.
A squirrel wears a tiny hat,
While crows perform a silly spat.

The flowers giggle as they sway,
Beneath the sun, they seize the day.
A rabbit pranks a sleepy cat,
Then hops away, imagine that!

Bees buzz loud with tales to tell,
Of honey jars and silly spells.
The pathway bends with every turn,
With antics, oh, we truly learn!

So in this maze of joyful glee,
Nature's quirks are plain to see.
A joyful tune in sunlight beams,
Awake we are in bramble dreams!

Whirlwinds of Wilding

When wildflowers twirl in the breeze,
They seem to laugh, if you please.
A tortoise wins a race, oh dear,
While ants march on without a fear.

The butterflies wear fancy shoes,
Unaware of impending snooze.
A gopher pops up with a grin,
Pulling weeds, bedecked in sin.

Oh, the whirlwind of mischief so bright,
Brambles laughing into the night.
The owls hoot with a cheeky cheer,
And whisper secrets, loud and clear.

In this chaos, joy does thrive,
With creatures bustling all alive.
So join the fun, don't miss the chance,
Where wilding spins in carefree dance!

The Glistening Dew's Secret

In morning's light, dew drops gleam,
A ladybug thinks it's a dream.
She rolls over, gives a yawn,
While daisies chuckle at the dawn.

A spider weaves a wobbly thread,
As beetles hum a tune instead.
They laugh and tease, "We're quite the crew!"
While ants march forth to steal the view.

Under the sun, all creatures play,
As squirrels chase their woes away.
The dew confesses in a sigh,
"Life's a jest! Come on, oh my!"

In this garden of wild delight,
Secrets sparkle, oh what a sight!
So gather 'round, take heart and cheer,
For life's the punchline, loud and clear!

Labyrinth of the Untamed

In a maze built of thorny delight,
Creatures scamper with all their might.
A porcupine dons fancy shoes,
While bushes giggle, spreading news.

The snails compete for slowest race,
With sprigs of parsley, they embrace.
A wild dance under the moon's light,
As shadows prance in sheer delight.

The paths weave round with clumsy grace,
Each nook and cranny's a new embrace.
A fox dons spectacles, quite absurd,
While whispers flutter, all unheard.

In this labyrinth, laughter flows,
Among the thickets, a secret grows.
So wander in, and let hearts roam,
Within the wild, you'll feel like home!

Ballads of the Hidden Grove

In a grove where shadows giggle,
A squirrel danced with a wiggle.
The owls hooted in delight,
As vines tangled in their flight.

Beneath the leaves, a rabbit sings,
Wearing tiny shoes with wings.
The bees buzzed a catchy tune,
While hatching plans to steal the moon.

The mushrooms hosted a grand rave,
Inviting all, both meek and brave.
Frogs leapt high, with leaps so bold,
As whispers of the night unfold.

Together they jested and played,
In a world where no one strayed.
With laughter echoing so bright,
In the hidden grove, pure delight.

Musings in the Grasp of Nature

On a branch, a wise old crow,
Told tall tales of antics low.
With acorns as his drink of choice,
He argued with a lively voice.

A hedgehog donned a tiny hat,
Tan and fluffy, just like that.
He rolled around, quite unaware,
Of the buzzing bees that dare.

In shade where the sunlight slips,
A bear is munching on some chips.
He sneezes loud, to everyone's glee,
Sending ants flying, oh dear me!

The laughter rings through leaf and vine,
In this place where all things align.
Nature hugs us, warm and tight,
As we revel in silly delight.

Letters from the Prickly Depths

A porcupine sent out a letter,
"Dear friends, I'm feeling much wetter!
Caught in raindrops, what a surprise,
I'll dry off under open skies!"

The fox replied with a grin so wide,
"I'll come over, let's go for a glide!
With puddles that splash and dance away,
Let's prance around, it's a fun day!"

A snail chimed in, in a slow, slick way,
"Just mind my trail, please, if you stay.
Those merry leaps might miss their mark,
And I'd hate to leave my treasure dark!"

In the depths where mischief thrives,
They share their laughs, the silliest jives.
Prickles and giggles, nature's sweet quirks,
In this patch of joy, joyfully lurks.

A Serenade of Twisted Branches

Underbranches twirled in cheer,
A raccoon strummed his banjo near.
With a wink, he played a tune,
Inviting fireflies to swoon.

A squirrel joined with acorn beats,
Creating rhythms on tiny feats.
With his tail, he led the dance,
While ants lined up in a trance.

The owls hooted, what a show!
Critters gathered, row by row.
With giggles bright, the night was theirs,
In tangled limbs, without a care.

As moonbeams twirled above their heads,
They laughed and danced on leafy beds.
In nature's heart, where fun enchants,
The branches swayed, with joyful prance.

Beneath the Canopy of Secrets

In thickets thick with sneaky vines,
I tripped on roots with funky designs.
A squirrel laughed, while I took a dive,
And vines whispered tales of the insects' hive.

A hedgehog rolled by, looking quite spry,
With a tiny top hat and a wink of his eye.
He offered me tea from a leaf-cupped pot,
I raised an eyebrow, thinking 'Why not?'

Beneath the leaves, where shadows play,
The raccoons dance in a merry ballet.
They juggled some berries, oh what a show,
And laughed as they tossed them, to and fro.

In that wild tangle, we all had fun,
Each critter a friend, no need to run.
I'll treasure these gigs beneath leafy skies,
In the land of laughter, where silliness lies.

Stories Woven with Briar Threads

In the tangled maze where stories unfold,
Lies a fable of critters both brave and bold.
A fox with a monocle, oh so dapper,
Sipped from a puddle, with dreams that caper.

A rabbit with glasses, quite scholarly keen,
Wrote his next novel titled, 'What is a Bean?'
With paws covered in ink and a tail all askew,
He muttered, 'This plot will leave them askew!'

The porcupine poet recited a rhyme,
About love found in the thickets, sublime.
But with every sharp quill, he'd poke a surprise,
As the audience chuckled and wiped their eyes.

In the embrace of thorns, laughter would rise,
With tales that grew wild like the greenest skies.
Every verse spun a world so absurdly bright,
In this brambly haven, all worries take flight.

Adventures in the Wild Tangle

In a patch of high grass where the butterflies zoom,
I found a snail planning a grand costume.
With glittery shells and a top hat, oh dear,
He proudly declared, 'I'm the king of this sphere!'

A game of hide and seek with a caterpillar,
As he tucked in his stripes, a colorful thriller.
He chuckled and whispered, 'Just look for my hat,
If I fit in the flowers, you won't see me, brat!'

A dirt path twisted through bushes so prime,
Where ants formed a line, synchronized in time.
They marched with a purpose, all little but proud,
While I cheered them on, oh how I laughed loud!

In this tangled adventure, with friends all around,
Every moment a treasure, forever unbound.
With giggles and pranks, the fun won't cease,
In this riot of nature, we found our peace.

Along the Winding Briarway

On a briarway winding through thorns and through leaves,

I met a posh owl, wearing fine weaves.
'Would you like some advice?' he hooted with flair,
'Never trust a hedgehog who claims he can share!'

A bear in a bowtie was throwing a feast,
With cake made of berries, he invited the least.
'Try my jam,' he grinned, with a twinkle of fun,
But it dripped down his chin, oh what a run!

Squirrels donned capes, as they swooped through the trees,
Confetti of acorns fluttered down like a breeze.
They giggled and chuckled, 'Watch us take flight!'
But crashed with a plump—their timing was light.

Amidst all the laughter, we lost track of the sun,
In this comical chaos, our hearts beat as one.
Along the briarway, where friendships ignite,
We danced through the thorns, till the stars took their flight.

Whispers Beneath the Thorny Veil

In the garden where mischief grows,
A hedgehog sneezes, and off it goes!
Bumblebees giggle, as they buzz so low,
While the dandelions dance in a playful row.

In the thicket, a rabbit tells a joke,
A snail chuckles, nearly broke!
The sly fox chuckles, sharp teeth agleam,
While the shy tortoise hides, caught in a dream.

Secrets of the Twisted Vines

Amidst the chaos of tangled greens,
A raccoon plots with mischievous schemes.
The wrinkled leaves whisper silly lore,
While squirrels chatter, always wanting more.

A vine wraps round a wandering shoe,
Laughter erupts from the flower crew.
No secret safe beneath the bright sun,
For giggles and grins are for everyone!

Echoes from the Wildwood

In the woods where shadows play,
An owl hoots, inviting foray.
Squirrels tumble from their lofty perch,
All for a nutty bread-baking search!

The trees are giggling, their limbs shaken,
A bear joins in, cracking jokes unspoken.
Who knew wildwood could be so bright?
With echoes of laughter filling the night!

Chronicles of Prickled Paths

On prickly paths where misfits roam,
A porcupine builds a tiny home.
He's grumpy yet wise, a prickly sage,
Tales of mishaps filling the page.

Dandelions puff, like clouds afloat,
While the toads croak a rickety note.
"Watch out for thorns!" the wise ones sing,
But laughter's the best gift that nature can bring!

Vignettes from the Overgrown Realm

In the jungle of my yard, oh what a sight,
Grasshoppers dance, what a comical flight!
A squirrel steals my lunch, what a cheeky thief,
I laugh as he scampers, my surprise turned disbelief.

Worms in tuxedos waltz on the leaf,
While ants hold a party, oh what a motif!
The dandelions giggle, waving 'hello,'
Each petal a jest, a whimsical show.

Through tangled vines and a maze of bloom,
I stumble and trip, but embrace the doom!
Laughter echoes beneath the sun's ray,
In this realm of weeds, I merrily stay.

A frog croaks sonnets, a melodic tune,
While bees hum along, a buzzing cartoon.
In this overgrown land filled with quirks,
Life's a silly romp, where nothing really works.

The Unraveled Thread of Nature

A spider spins tales, with webbing so neat,
Trapping wayward flies for a not-so-fine treat.
Yet slips through the cracks, a dollop of cream,
My breakfast entangled in her sticky dream.

The squirrels plot mischief, each caper a jest,
Stealing birdseed ungraciously, they're truly the best!
A chipmunk observes with a knowing grin,
While I plan my lawn escape, under my chin.

The wind tells a secret, a mischievous breeze,
Whispers to blossoms, causing them to sneeze.
A fit of laughter erupts from a tree,
As leaves shake and tremble, in giggly decree.

Days unravel like yarn on a playful cat's quest,
Nature's a comedian, at her wildest and best.
With each thorny episode, I'm bound to fall,
Embrace the absurd, in this verdant brawl.

In the Embrace of the Thorny Path

Walking through thickets, I stumble and trip,
A thistle's sharp poke, oh, what a cruel whip!
The bushes are laughing, as I test my skill,
Nature's own obstacle course gives me a thrill.

A hedgehog rolls by, quite suddenly bold,
Wearing a mask, he's the knight of the cold!
In this odd ballad, we dance without grace,
While a butterfly giggles, at our clumsy embrace.

A fox plays it cool, tail flipping in jest,
While I navigate brambles, at nature's behest.
He winks and he prances, I can't help but snort,
As he leads me astray, I'm more lost than sport.

Yet every sharp turn brings a chuckle, it's true,
In this prickly kingdom, I feel born anew.
Through laughter and chaos, I find my own path,
As I forge through the thorns, avoiding the wrath!

Seasons of the Winding Trail

Spring blooms with laughter, in technicolor flair,
Petunias gossip while waxing their hair.
A robin rehearses for nature's grand play,
Chasing me off as I wander astray.

Summer bursts forth, a party galore,
Bees buzzing tunes while I duck and I pour!
Lemonade spills as I slip on a dew,
In this muggy mirth, giggles sprout anew.

Autumn arrives, in a shower of leaves,
Each crackling footstep an ode as it weaves.
Raccoons wear their masks, planning midnight steals,
While I grin and dance, embraced by their reels.

Winter retreats in its flurry and chill,
A snowman chuckles, a figure of thrill.
With laughter in cycles, the trails intertwine,
In the seasons' warm grip, I revel, divine!

Rhapsody of the Wild Undergrowth

In the garden of squawks and fuzzy bees,
Little bugs argue, 'Who ate my cheese?'
A squirrel in shades struts with such bravado,
While ants form a conga, good luck to the trio.

Beneath the wild leaves, a curious toad,
Sings off-key love songs on his muddy road.
The ladybug giggles, her friends in a row,
While the thistle looks on, like a grumpy old foe.

The wind rustles softly, stirring up cheer,
As a bear on a diet steals honey, oh dear!
The rabbits debate about carrots in hand,
In this wild, tangled mess, no one can quite stand.

Yet in this mishmash, laughter does bloom,
As a critter parade turns the gloom into room.
Oh, the tales of the undergrowth weave and spin,
Where chaos reigns free, it's the wild's original sin.

Murmurs of the Blackberry Path

On the path where the blackberries mix with the dew,
A hedgehog in spectacles reads self-help for two.
He claims it's quite crucial to manage his spines,
While the crows cluck with laughter at such bold designs.

A rabbit with dreams of becoming a star,
Practices lines with the voice of a jar.
'There's more to this life than just munching on greens,'
He proclaims as he hops, with two squirrels in jeans.

A fox paints a mural with berries and zest,
While chipmunks debate which snack is the best.
The whispers of mischief float close to the ground,
As bees waltz around, making sweet, buzzing sounds.

Around every corner, a giggle or shout,
As nature's own sitcom plays out all about.
With joy in the brambles, where silliness thrives,
The berries tell secrets; oh, what a life!

Chronicles of the Unseen Wilderness

In the thicket of shadows, a raccoon with flair,
Hides treasures of snacks with the utmost of care.
His laugh echoes softly through branches so lush,
As he shares with a turtle who's knitting a brush.

There's a hedgehog who juggles with acorns so round,
While a cat in a cape pretends he can sound.
The whispers of mischief bounce high in the trees,
As a badger plays drums, oh flow, sweet melodies!

With critters disguised as they role-play with fun,
A mouse in a crown declares they've all won!
Each story they share is a giggle-filled tune,
Under soft, watchful eyes of the cheeky raccoon.

In the heart of the clutter, where secrets entwine,
The laughter of nature fills every line.
These chronicles spin through the wild and the free,
In the unseen wilderness, pure harmony.

Where the Brambles Waver

Where the brambles waver and wiggle with glee,
A hedgehog and worm share a cup of sweet tea.
They toast to the day, and they giggle out loud,
While a sly little fox claims the tea party crowd.

A deer on a skateboard zooms past with a grin,
Chasing after his dreams like a whirlwind of din.
And over the hill, a flock of geese squawk,
Debating their fashion while taking a walk.

The thistles all chuckle as butterflies dance,
While sunflowers gossip about romance.
A hedgehog's advice: "Just be who you are!"
And a raccoon's reply: "I've got dreams; let's go far!"

In a world where each creature has joy to unearth,
They find funny moments that truly hold worth.
So gather your pals for a mess that's a caper,
In the brambles, where laughter's the ultimate paper.

Mythos of the Hidden Boughs

In the thicket where whispers dance,
A squirrel steals my secret stance.
With acorns grand, he struts around,
Claiming treasures that he found.

Beneath the leaves, I spy a fox,
Wearing shades and mismatched socks.
He nods at me, a knowing grin,
In this wild realm, we're kin, not sin.

A mockingbird sings out of tune,
Belting notes under the moon.
I chuckle, wondering what it means,
A song for squirrels, or just for beans?

In tangled roots, adventures seek,
With mischief that makes us all weak.
Among the branches, laughter grows,
In hidden realms where silliness flows.

Rhapsody of the Rustic Hedge

In the hedge where gnomes reside,
There's a party none can hide.
With tiny hats and tiny beers,
They dance with joy and silly cheers.

A hedgehog waltzes with great flair,
In polka dots, without a care.
He tips his hat, then points his nose,
To all the blooms in splendid rows.

The bumblebees buzz a big beat,
While ants parade and don tiny feet.
They march in line, proud and straight,
Feeling grand on this wild estate.

I watch them swirl, I see them twirl,
Each creature gives the day a whirl.
A raucous song in every bend,
In this hedge, fun has no end.

Meditations Amongst the Wild Flora

In flower patches, thoughts collide,
With petals soft, they tend to hide.
A butterfly fluffs up his wing,
And hoots like owls, what a wild thing!

The daisies gossip, oh so coy,
For dandelions, life's a joy.
They share the tales of who's the best,
While grasshoppers jump, put to the test.

Tiny ants boast of their great weight,
As snail attempts a speedy skate.
Their slow and steady, quick and spry,
Create a circus 'neath the sky.

I lounge on clovers, take a gander,
The wilds are filled with pure meander.
Each laugh and jest, a lesson learned,
In this quirky world, my spirit's turned.

Enigmas of the Flourishing Wilds

In blooming fields, the secrets weave,
With whispers caught in every leave.
A rabbit hops in puzzlement,
As wise old owl looks heaven-sent.

The thorns confide their prickly jokes,
While roses laugh with all the folks.
Petunias giggle, violets snort,
As bees partake in their witty court.

A cactus sings a high-pitched tune,
To rocks that roll under the moon.
They sway and hum atop the knoll,
In these wilds, they play their role.

I join the fun, with sparks to share,
In these mysteries, none declare.
With nature's jest, we play along,
In flourishing bliss, we all belong.

Secrets of the Gnarled Path

In the woods where shadows dance,
Footwear tangled in a prance.
The trees chuckle, leaves conspire,
While squirrels plot and spark their fire.

A hedgehog winks, then rolls away,
With acorns as his grand buffet.
Roots become the jester's joke,
As branches break in laughter's poke.

Fungi sprout with faces wide,
Grinning as they mock the tide.
The paths may twist, but we'll not fret,
For every stumble, there's humor yet.

Embers of Lost Wanderings

A rabbit hops, a tumble here,
His nose a-twitch, no hint of fear.
With every leap, a story spun,
Of trails uncharted, and yet so fun.

The fireflies giggle, lighting the scene,
As invisible sprites engage in a routine.
They twirl and whirl, in glittering cheer,
Guiding our feet, with nothing to fear.

We chase after shadows, keen on delight,
With sleepy badgers, tucked in for the night.
Each wrong turn leads to something grand,
In the dance of the wayward, life is unplanned.

The Berry-Picked Melodies

Strawberries sing from the vine's tight embrace,
While bluesh berries bop with a jiggly grace.
The raspberries giggle in red-coated glee,
As they plot against the ants sipping tea.

A chubby finch comes, with songs in his beak,
He stumbles on berries, oh what a sneak!
With each little hop, he steals with a flair,
Cracking a smile on the old garden chair.

The fruits spin tales of daytime delight,
As bees buzz around, a curious sight.
For each berry's burst brings laughter in throngs,
In the jumbled chorus of life's silly songs.

Reflections in the Briar

In a tangle of thorns lies a mirror so neat,
It catches your face, and shows two left feet.
With brambles to guide, and a thicket's jest,
Who knew nature's laugh was truly the best?

A crow caws loud at the bushes, they quip,
"Your hat's on backwards, just let it slip!"
But the shadows hum softly, a tune so absurd,
While worms weave tales that are utterly blurred.

So swagger along, with mishaps and cheer,
For life's little jests are what we hold dear.
In this tangled web, take a moment to pause,
And dance with the shadows, give them applause.

Whimsy in the Choked Underbrush

In tangled greens, a squirrel schemes,
He's plotting a heist, or so it seems.
With acorns stacked up high in tow,
He trips on roots, oh, what a show!

A rabbit hops with an awkward flair,
Wearing a hat—who knows how rare?
He giggles softly, a silly sight,
As he munches greens by the pale moonlight.

The hedgehogs hold a grand parade,
With tiny drums they've cleverly made.
They march in step, though all askew,
Nature's jesters, making do!

And when the sunlight starts to fade,
The critters dance, unafraid.
In the brambles, laughter reigns,
As joy spills forth from hidden lanes.

Legends of the Verdant Snare

Deep in the boughs, a rumor flies,
A toad sings tales of bigger lies.
He croaks of dragons who lost their scales,
And of mice who rode on ancient whales.

The foxes nod with knowing grins,
As legends twist, like tangled pins.
A snail claims he swam in a sea,
But really just hid behind a tree.

The beetles hold a trivia night,
With questions that tickle, and answers slight.
"Who wears a crown made of fallen leaves?"
"Is it the owl or the puffball that grieves?"

Yet when the moon lifts high and bright,
The forest laughs till the morning light.
In the thicket, all's pure delight,
As tales of folly take their flight.

Heartbeats Beneath the Thorns

In the bristly club of thorns and leaves,
A lovebird sings, and never deceives.
He woos a lass with a fruity tune,
But trips on a twig, oh, what a swoon!

A pair of badgers in their stylish wear,
Swap stories of fashion, decently rare.
They prance and pose, so filled with glee,
Until one rolls down, now isn't that free?

The fireflies flicker, like tiny stars,
They laugh at the frogs in their silly cars.
With laughter echoing through the glades,
They race and bump, in amusing parades!

Thus beats the heart of this wild, bright land,
With friends entwined, oh so unplanned.
In a realm where joy takes its form,
Each heartbeat brings life to the norm.

Soliloquies of the Leafy Labyrinth

Through the twisted paths of tangled greens,
The wise old owl shares his musings keen.
"Why did the chicken cross the bramble?
To scratch her itch, or just to ramble?"

A lizard lounges with flair and style,
Basking in sun, he grins with a guile.
He jests about the ants so small,
"Just wait till they attempt to haul!"

Dandelions sway in the teasing breeze,
With jokes whispered through rustling leaves.
The flowers giggle, mischief at play,
As bees buzz nonsense throughout the day.

So here amidst the tangle and twist,
Nature's humor we cannot resist.
The labyrinth thrives with chuckles untold,
In the leafy embrace, life sings bold.

Twists of Fate in the Greenwood

In a thicket thick with chatter,
Came a squirrel with dreams to scatter.
He aimed to fly, with a leaf for a wing,
But crash-landed hard, oh what a thing!

A rabbit donned a foolish grin,
Watching the chaos that would soon begin.
"Join me for noodle soup!" he did shout,
But found himself stuck in a muddled route.

A turtle prized speed beyond the sun,
With roller skates, he thought it was fun.
But kicked up dirt and caused quite a stir,
Tripped on a root, oh what a blur!

In the woods, laughter surely grows,
Among lovely friends and their funny woes.
With every twist and silly mistake,
Life's humdrum days become a piece of cake!

The Enchanted Tangle

Deep in the woods where mischief sprouts,
A fox wore shoes to dance about.
He slipped and slid right past a tree,
As a hare laughed out, "Dance, you silly bee!"

A chatting bird with gossip to share,
Told of a frog who thought he could swear.
He croaked a tune that sounded quite odd,
And all the bugs bowed, giving a nod.

Then came a breeze with a tickling touch,
Sending the leaves in a spin too much.
A mysterious voice sang a silly rhyme,
The animals chuckled till the end of time.

So in this tangle, where giggles ignite,
Each twist and turn brings sheer delight.
For those who wander and take a chance,
Will find magic tucked in a woodland dance!

Stories Embedded in Twigs

In the bed of the forest, wisdom resides,
A wise old owl, with twisty sides.
He recounted tales of misfit creatures,
Who all wore mishaps as quirky features.

A hedgehog fashioned a hat from a shoe,
Declared himself judge at a dance-off too!
But pricked by fame, he spun in place,
Fell flat on his back, what an amusing case!

The porcupine brought a snack quite bizarre,
A cake made from berries, all covered in tar.
When invited to feast, guests all took a bite,
Then burst into giggles, a delightful sight!

So gather round for the tales yet untold,
In every little twig, a new laugh unfolds.
For life in the woods is a raucous affair,
With stories embedded that dance in the air!

Beneath the Canopy: A Silent Dialogue

Under the boughs where secrets dwell,
A pair of raccoons had much to tell.
With whispers and giggles, they shared a snack,
But one snatched a cookie, what a comical crack!

Above, a crow with a sparkle of sass,
Watched as the mischief began to amass.
"Is that cookie fresh, or a month out of date?"
The raccoons just froze, debating their fate.

Meanwhile, a snail trailed a sparkling line,
Mocking the chaos, feeling just fine.
"I'll make it by dinner, just you wait and see!"
With laughter so loud, a call from the tree.

So beneath the canopy, laughter takes flight,
In a ballet of blunders, all pure delight.
For in the wild, each heart finds a song,
In silly dialogues where all feel they belong!

The Tangle of Untold Stories

In a patch of thorns so bright,
Looming shadows dance at night.
Squirrels knit with glee, oh wow!
They soon forget just how to bow.

With berries squished in funny ways,
And stories tangled in the maze.
A fox with flair, a cheeky grin,
Claims he's lost, oh where's he been?

Jokes are tossed like leaves in flight,
The gossip spreads, it feels so right.
In this garden full of cheer,
Laughter lingers, drawing near.

Bramble beasts in fancy hats,
Tickle each other, giggle like cats.
Each thorn a punchline, every twist,
In stories lurking, close to twist.

Memories Woven in the Green

In shades of green, a tale unfolds,
Of whispers shared and laughs retold.
A hedgehog juggles acorns bright,
While crickets chirp, oh what a sight!

They reminisce of days gone by,
Where clumsy bees could barely fly.
A dance of petals, a breeze so sweet,
With every turn, there's more to meet.

The dandelions boast of flights,
Of trouble stirred on cozy nights.
They scheme and dream without a care,
Beneath the sun, there's joy to share.

Twists of yarn from tail to toe,
Each memory stitched, in ebb and flow.
What fun we'll have, they cheer and sing,
In a wild world where laughter clings!

Threads of Nature's Weave

In tangled threads of nature's play,
The bugs hold court, and never sway.
A spider spins with crafty hands,
Telling tales of distant lands.

With sunlit rays and whispers soft,
The leaves exchange their secrets oft.
A rabbit hides with painted nails,
While laughter echoes through the trails.

Mice dance waltzes on the grass,
While cheeky frogs, all class, alas!
With cloven feet, they jump and prance,
In every twist a chance to dance.

The seasons twine, a comedic spin,
As laughter bursts like blossoms in.
In every cranny, smiles abide,
In tangled tales, for joy's our guide!

Lullabies of Briars

In briar beds, where secrets lie,
The nightingale sings, oh my, oh my!
With lullabies that tickle the ear,
And whispers shared that dance with beer.

A raccoon in a midnight trench,
Finds magic berries, oh what a wench!
Together they cram, oh what a sight,
In shadowy laughter 'til morning light.

A hedgehog hums a tune so sweet,
As furry friends tap their tiny feet.
With magic mushrooms, they take a leap,
In dreams of berries, each shall keep.

Through briars bold, they twist and twirl,
In the moonlit night, such chaos unfurl.
With every snicker in a weary sigh,
They cradle their dreams as stars float by!

Whispers Among Thorned Vines

In the garden where mischief plays,
Thorns tickle, turning good to gray.
A hedgehog sings a silly tune,
While the bumblebees buzz in June.

Lurking around, a squirrel's delight,
Hiding acorns, oh what a sight!
Raccoons debate on late-night snacks,
While the moonlight glimmers on their tracks.

Giggling flowers dance in the breeze,
Tickled pink by the buzzing bees.
Even the weeds join in the fun,
Under the warmth of the golden sun.

So tiptoe gently, laugh without care,
For in this garden, joy's everywhere!
Among the thorns, laughter invites,
Planting memories on moonlit nights.

Shadows of Wild Growth

In shadows deep where creatures creep,
The shadows chatter and secrets seep.
A lizard slips in a competitive race,
While crickets gossip, hopping place to place.

Among the ferns, a snail takes a peek,
Wearing a shell, a fashion unique.
The owl hoots in a high-pitched tone,
While the fox pretends he's all alone.

Plants tussle and tussle; they bicker and fight,
Over sunlight, oh what a sight!
Beetles bring popcorn to a grand feast,
While the grasshoppers prance, never ceased.

So if you wander past the wild cling,
Listen closely to the gossip they bring.
Through laughter and chaos, they weave their lore,
In tangled whispers behind nature's door.

Echoes in the Thicket

In thick brush where echoes play,
Something silly lurks in the fray.
A hedgehog jigs, a dance of glee,
As branches swish like a bumblebee.

Frogs croak tunes, a lively band,
While raccoons giggle, popcorn in hand.
Even the trees join in on fun,
Twisting and turning under the sun.

Bouncing deer play tag with the mist,
Ignoring the rules, you get the gist.
Waves of laughter ripple the air,
In this haven of joy, without a care.

So if you hear laughter from the brink,
Join the party, take a moment to think.
For in the thicket, where echoes entwine,
Life's a great joke, and it's yours to define.

Secrets Underneath the Leaves

Beneath the leaves, secrets reside,
Where worms wiggle and critters hide.
A sleeping snail dreams of a race,
While ants march on, steady their pace.

A chubby badger rolls with flair,
As butterflies dance in a state of fair.
Raindrops giggle, splashing around,
Creating puddles, joyous and round.

The hedges rustle with whispers low,
As frogs and toads put on a show.
Mice hold meetings, planning their quests,
While the bushes play, "Who does it best?"

Laughter and secrets, a wild charade,
Nature's theater, beautifully laid.
So when you wander through rustling leaves,
Join in the fun, let your heart believe!

Hidden Beneath the Petals and Thorns

In a garden where mischief resides,
A snail once claimed he could glide.
He slid on a leaf, oh what a sight,
Then tripped on a twig, quite the flight!

The daisies all giggled, they couldn't believe,
CHuckle-worthy moments that never deceive.
A frog with a crown croaked a tune,
While ants in a row danced under the moon.

A butterfly swirled, with flair and with style,
Luring a bee to stay for a while.
But the bee, oh dear, had a sweet tooth too strong,
And soon he was buzzing a peculiar song.

So here in this chaos, a comedy played,
With each tiny creature, a role they displayed.
Life's whims in the garden, a playful charade,
Where laughter and blooms are a joyful cascade.

The Wild Portrait of a Life

In a thicket where shadows and sunlight converge,
Lives a hedgehog with dreams that emerge.
He wishes to fly, to soar up so high,
But rolls into a bush at the first sign of sky.

A rabbit with spectacles looks ever so wise,
Thinks carrots can teach him the secrets of skies.
He scribbles on napkins with thoughts on the breeze,
While squirrels just giggle, 'He's lost in the trees!'

A wild art show held by the bees in a jar,
With honey as paint; oh, they've raised the bar!
But the flies came to critic, wings buzzing in glee,
'We find it quite sweet, but too sticky for me!'

Yet amid all the chaos, smiles gleam true bright,
With laughter and friendship, everything's right.
In the wild portrait of life, we find our own way,
With quirks and with giggles that brighten the day.

The Thicket's Fabled Whisper

In the thicket, whispers come and go,
A tale of a cat who danced with a crow.
He stumbled on twigs, and they giggled aloud,
As he twirled in a circle, so fun, so proud!

A tortoise once challenged the speed of a hare,
Said, 'With patience, my friend, I'll take you somewhere!'

But the hare fell asleep by a dandelion,
While the tortoise munched leaves, supremely defying.

Then came a wise owl, with spectacles on,
Telling tall tales from dusk until dawn.
He hooted of treasures, of riches untold,
But all that they found was a sock—how bold!

In the thicket's embrace, where laughter's the norm,
Each creature creates, a whimsical swarm.
With stories that twist 'round joyfully thick,
Together they weave a comedic schtick.

Riddles in the Briary Maze

In a briar maze, riddles twist and turn,
A fox with a hat, his wisdom to learn.
He asked of a worm, who correctly replied,
'What's faster than light? Oh, just look inside!'

A crow cawed with laughter, 'What can I say?
These questions are silly and lead you astray!
But say, little fox, come play a game,
A riddle in riddles, we'll both share the fame.'

So off they did prance through paths of green light,
Fumbling on words, causing giggles so bright.
Beneath every thorn lay a chuckle or cheer,
Where each twist of the tale drew them nearer in fear.

The maze full of folly, where every turn's fun,
With quips exchanged freely 'til day turned to done.
In riddles and laughter that echoes their play,
In this briary labyrinth, they chase blues away.

www.ingramcontent.com/pod-product-compliance
Lightning Source LLC
Chambersburg PA
CBHW071845160426
43209CB00003B/424